The Wild Side of Pet Rabbits

Jo Waters

Chicago, Illinois

For information, address the publisher:
Raintree, 100 N. LaSalle, Suite 1200
Chicago, IL 60602
Customer Service: 888-363-4266
Visit our website at www.raintreelibrary.com

Printed and bound in China by South China Printing Company.
09 08 07 06 05
10 9 8 7 6 5 4 3 2 1

Library of Congress Cataloging-in-Publication Data
Waters, Jo.
  The wild side of pet rabbits / Jo Waters.
     p. cm. -- (Wild Side of Pets)
  Includes bibliographical references and index.
  ISBN 1-4109-1409-7 (library binding-hardcover) -- ISBN 1-4109-1415-1 (pbk.)
 1. Rabbits. I. Title. II. Series: Waters, Jo. Wild side of pets.
  SF453.W38 2005
  636.932'2--dc22

Acknowledgments
The publishers would like to thank the following for permission to reproduce photographs: Ardea pp. **9**, **23**, **26**, **27** (John Daniels); Corbis p. **16**; FLPA p. **14**, **28**; Getty Images p. **29** (Photodisc); Nature Picture Library pp. **22** (David Kjaer) **24** (T.J. Rich); NHPA pp. **4** (Mike Lane) **5** (Alan Williams) **6** (Rod Planck) **20** (Manfred Danegger); OSF p. **10** (G I Bernard); Tudor Photography/Harcourt Education Ltd pp. **5**, **7**, **11** (Mike Farrell) **13**, **15**, **17** (Mike Farrell) **19**, **21** (Mike Farrell) **25**.

Cover photograph of white and brown pet rabbit reproduced with permission of Ardea (Johan de Meester). Inset Photograph of a rabbit in a burrow reproduced with permission of OSF.

The publishers would like to thank Michaela Miller for her assistance in the preparation of this book.

Every effort has been made to contact copyright holders of any material reproduced in this book. Any omissions will be rectified in subsequent printings if notice is given to the publishers.

The paper used to print this book comes from sustainable resources.

Contents

Any words appearing in bold, **like this**, are explained in the glossary.

Was Your Pet Once Wild?

You may think that you just have a pet rabbit, but the rabbits people keep as pets are very close to their wild relatives. Finding out more about the wild side of your pet will help you give it a better life.

Family

*Did you know that rabbits, hares, cottontails, and **pikas** are all related to each other?*

There are many different types of rabbit in the wild.

Rabbits have been kept by people since the time of Ancient Rome. Two thousand years ago the Romans spread across Europe. They took their **domesticated** rabbits with them to these areas.

Rabbits make good pets because they are **sociable** animals. They enjoy company. They need everyday care, so you must be able to spend time with them.

Pet rabbits (top) and wild rabbits (bottom) are closely related.

Types of Rabbit

There are about 30 different types of wild rabbit. These include European rabbits and African rabbits. There are also many different **species** of American rabbits called cottontails.

Size
Wild British rabbits usually only grow to about 4 pounds (2 kilograms) Canadian Arctic hares can grow up to 11 pounds (5 kilograms).

Hares and **pikas** are also part of the rabbit family. Hares are bigger than rabbits and have longer legs and ears. Pikas are small and have round ears. They are also known as rock rabbits.

Desert cottontails have soft brown fur that blends in with the sand and earth.

6

Pet rabbits are similar to wild rabbits, but they are **domesticated**. There are a lot of different **breeds** of pet rabbits. Most are **descended** from the wild European rabbit, even in Australia and North America. Many people moved to Australia and North America from Europe and brought their animals with them.

The British Giant is one of the biggest rabbit breeds in the world!

Pet rabbits come in all sorts of shapes and sizes. **Dwarf** rabbits such as the Polish dwarf may weigh less than 2 pounds (about a kilogram). In contrast, Flemish giants can weigh over 20 pounds (9 kilograms).

Where Are Rabbits From

Rabbits and hares live in most countries across the world. They can be found across Europe and northwest Africa as well as in parts of South America and Australia.

In Australia farmers think that rabbits are **pests** because they eat and destroy so much grass and crops.

Hares live in North America, Europe, and Asia. Cottontails only live in North and South America.

This map shows where wild rabbits can be found.

Choosing your pet

If you decide that a rabbit is the right pet for you, make sure to get your rabbit from a good **breeder**. Never buy animals that have been caught from the wild. This is cruel to the rabbit.

When you are choosing your rabbit you should make sure it is healthy. It should have bright eyes and be alert. It should have neat teeth and claws and a glossy coat. Ask to handle the rabbit to find out how tame it is.

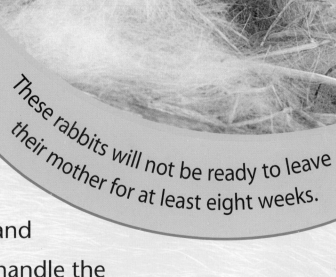

These rabbits will not be ready to leave their mother for at least eight weeks.

Rabbit Habitats

Wild rabbits live on grasslands and plains. Some also live in fields, sand dunes, and forests. Rabbits like sandy or chalky areas best because they are the easiest to dig in.

Rabbits live in underground burrows called warrens. There is a main living chamber. There is also a nest chamber lined with fur and grass to make it soft for babies. Lots of tunnels lead out of the chambers.

The burrows have escape passages in case a **predator** comes underground.

Housing

Pet rabbits need a large hutch to live in. You can keep your rabbit hutch indoors or outdoors. It should keep your rabbit warm, dry, and sheltered.

Runs

Your pet also needs exercise. An outdoor cage called a run lets your pet run around and eat fresh grass. It should have wire mesh on the top, sides, and bottom so the rabbit cannot escape and nothing else can get in.

The best bedding is wood shavings with a little hay. Hay keeps the rabbits warm and they can nibble it, too.

Rabbit Anatomy

Wild rabbits have round bodies, long back legs, and large feet. They have shorter front legs, long ears, and large front teeth for **gnawing** and eating. Wild rabbits and hares also have short fluffy tails. In the United States, "cottontails" got their name because of their white, furry tails.

Rabbits have teeth that never stop growing. In the wild they wear their teeth down by chewing grass and tough twigs.

This drawing shows the skeleton of a rabbit.

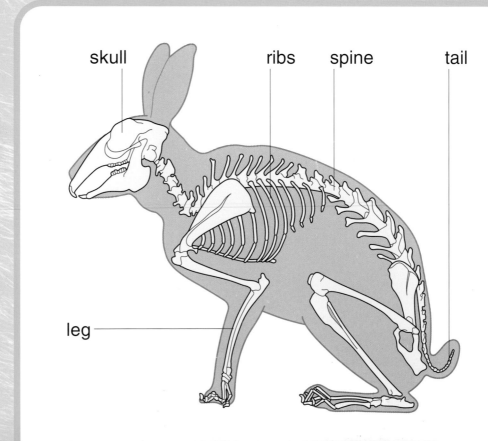

skull   ribs   spine   tail

leg

Pet rabbits have the same **anatomy** as wild ones. But **breeders** have bred pet rabbits to make many shapes and sizes, from **dwarfs** to giants. There are also a lot of coat colors and lengths.

How to pick up a rabbit

Never pick up rabbits by their ears. Put one hand under the bottom to support the rabbit and hold the front legs and paws gently with the other.

Make sure you always hold your rabbit with both hands.

Senses

Wild rabbits have very sensitive senses, especially sight and hearing.

They have large eyes at the sides of their heads. This allows them to look out for danger all around them. They can even see behind themselves!

Hearing is very important to rabbits for sensing danger. They also use their hearing for **communication**. Rabbits thump the ground with a back leg to warn of danger. When the other rabbits hear this they all run and hide.

Rabbits use sight and hearing to avoid **predators** in the wild and to find food.

Pet rabbits use the same senses as their wild relatives. They use their sight to find their way around their homes. They are very curious and like to smell everything. If you let your rabbit run free in your house it will probably hop around and sniff things for a while to see what is new.

Quiet!
Rabbits have very sensitive hearing and don't like much noise. Even music can make them unhappy and stressed. Make sure you keep them somewhere quiet.

Rabbits seem to enjoy listening to their owners, so sit and talk quietly to them sometimes!

Movement

Rabbits and hares use their muscles to move. They hop instead of walking or running. Their long back feet and powerful back legs help them to jump and move at high speed.

Boxing

Hares box in spring, when it is the mating season. They stand up on their hind legs and fight with their front legs.

Hares can run very quickly, up to 50 miles (80 kilometers) per hour! The snowshoe hare has big fluffy feet with toes that spread out. These help it to cross soft snow without sinking in.

Snowshoe hares can jump up to 9 ft (3 m) in one hop!

Rabbits need to go in a run or to be let out every day.

Exercising

Pet rabbits also use their long back feet and powerful hind legs to hop. They use their shorter front legs for balance.

Pet rabbits need plenty of space to exercise in their hutch and outdoor run. Rabbits should always be able to move around comfortably in their hutches as well.

What Do Rabbits Eat?

Wild rabbits and hares eat grass and leaves like clover and herbs. They also chew bark and nibble young trees. Sometimes they eat berries and fruit, too.

In the wild, rabbits have **adapted** to eat a lot of different foods. This is because they have to eat whatever is growing. In summer there is a lot of fresh grass and **vegetation**. In the fall there are fruits and berries, but in winter fewer foods can grow.

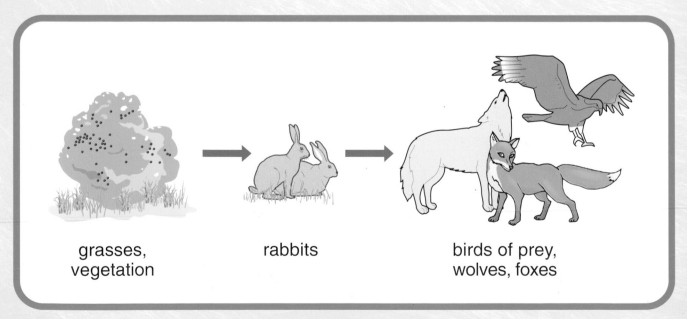

| grasses, vegetation | rabbits | birds of prey, wolves, foxes |

Rabbits fit into a **food chain** like this.

Pet rabbits cannot find their own food like wild rabbits, so you must feed them. You can get special rabbit food from pet stores.

Eating droppings

*Rabbits **digest** their food twice. They eat their droppings to get all the nutrition out of them.*

Rabbits love dandelion leaves, grass, carrots, celery, apples, and even kiwi fruits. But don't give rabbits lettuce, it can make them sick.

Your rabbit should always have a supply of clean water. A water dropper bottle is the best way to give water.

Your rabbit should also have nice hay and fresh vegetables.

Foraging and Playing

Wild rabbits and hares are very active most of the time. They search for food and stay alert for danger. They are **herbivores**, so they do not hunt for food, but they do have to **forage** for fresh grass and **vegetation**.

Young rabbits play with their brothers and sisters. Playing makes their muscles stronger and helps them learn how to survive when they grow up. It also helps rabbits learn about **communicating** with others.

Wild rabbits are curious and like to find out about things.

You can make feeding time for your pet rabbit more like it would be in the wild. Scatter its food around the hutch or outdoor run and let the rabbit find it.

Pet rabbits can also eat grass if you let them out in a run. Foraging in the yard or run will give your rabbit plenty of exercise and keep it happy.

Rabbits also like having toys. They enjoy playing with wooden balls or shapes.

Toys like tunnels and flower pots keep your rabbit fit and active.

Do Rabbits Live in Groups?

Wild rabbits live in groups and are very **sociable**. Rabbit groups have a **hierarchy**. This means that in a rabbit group, each rabbit has a job.

The boss rabbits are the strongest and they look after the rest of the rabbits. Some rabbits guard the others, watching over the warren and warning if danger is near.

Living alone

Most rabbits live in groups, but hares and some cottontails are different. They usually live alone or in pairs, only coming together when they **mate**.

These rabbits are guarding their warren.

Just like wild rabbits, pet rabbits need company. A pair of two males or two females is best. A male and a female rabbit will also get along well. But make sure they are **neutered** so they do not mate and have babies.

If your rabbits have not grown up together, you must introduce them carefully to make sure they get along. Otherwise they may fight.

Grooming your pet rabbit is a great way to show your friendship. Your pet rabbit will probably try to groom you back!

If you can, it is best to keep more than one rabbit.

23

Sleeping

European and Australian rabbits sleep in their burrows. They are **diurnal**, which means they sleep during most of the day and night. They are awake around dawn and dusk. They do not come out much during the day, but they do come out more at night.

Wild rabbits and hares all need to sleep, but they do not all dig burrows. Cottontails rest in long grass or under bushes. Hares do not dig burrows either. They build nests, called forms, in long grass.

This hare is having a rest in his form.

Most pet rabbits are diurnal too. This means they will be awake in the mornings and evenings, so you can play with them and let them exercise.

But just like their wild relatives, they need to be able to rest during the day as well. Their hutch or run should have a special sleeping area where they can curl up safe and sound. It is good to give them some soft hay to burrow into.

Pet rabbits also need to rest and sleep.

Life Cycle of Rabbits

Rabbits, hares, and cottontails live for different lengths of time. European rabbits can live for about nine years. Most only live for about five years as they have so many **predators**. Hares can live for twelve years, but in the wild they usually live for around four years.

Rabbits and cottontails give birth to naked, blind babies. Rabbit babies are called kittens. Hare babies are called leverets. They are born with fur and with open eyes. Hares have about two or three babies in a litter.

Rabbit kittens have no fur when they are born.

A male rabbit is called a buck and a female is called a doe.

Rabbits **breed** very easily. Unlike wild rabbits, pet rabbits can breed all year round. Rabbits are usually pregnant for about 31 days.

Neutering

*Both male and female pet rabbits can be **neutered** to stop them from having babies. It also makes the rabbits calmer, so they get along better with other rabbits.*

A doe can have between two and eight babies, but usually they have five or six.

Common Problems

Wild rabbits and hares are often eaten by **predators**. They are also hunted and eaten by people.

Farming and building destroy hare **habitats** so they have nowhere to live.

Wild rabbits can get a nasty disease called myxomatosis. This spreads quickly and kills infected rabbits.

Hundreds of bunnies
Rabbits are not in danger. In fact they are considered a **pest** *in places like Australia because there are so many of them.*

Australian farmers build special fences to keep rabbits out.

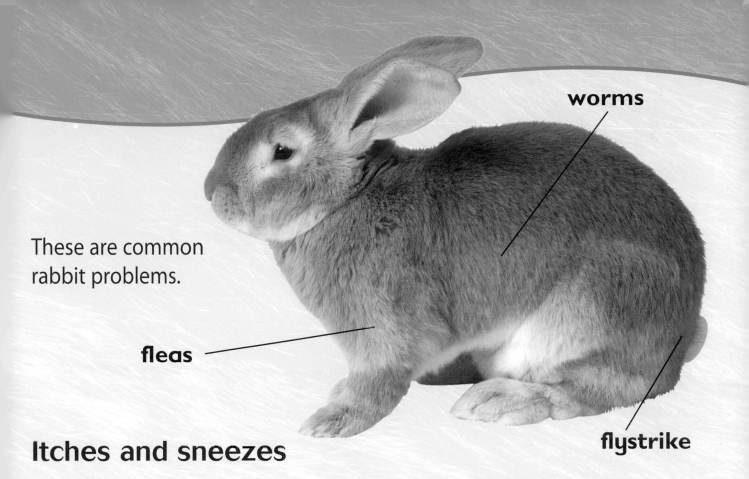

worms

These are common
rabbit problems.

fleas

flystrike

Itches and sneezes

Rabbits can get **parasites**. These include fleas, mites, or
ticks on their skin. They can get worms inside them, too.
Your veterinarian can treat parasites.

Rabbits can also get flystrike. Flies lay eggs on dirty fur,
which hatch into **maggots**. The maggots burrow under
the fur and can kill the rabbit. You can prevent this by
keeping your rabbit really clean.

Now you know more about why rabbits behave the
way they do, you can look forward to a rewarding
future with your pets.

Find Out for Yourself

A good owner will always want to learn more about keeping pet rabbits. To find out more information about rabbits, you can look in other books and on the Internet.

Books to read

Searle, Nancy. *Your Rabbit: A Kid's Guide to Raising and Showing.* Pownal, VT: Storey, 2003.

Rayner, Matthew, *et al. Rabbits.* Milwaukee: Garreth Stevens, 2004.

Using the Internet

Use a search engine, such as *www.yahooligans.com* or *www.internet4kids.com.* You could try searching using the key words "rabbit," "pet," and "wild rabbits."

Glossary

adapt become used to living in certain conditions

anatomy how the body is made

breed when two animals mate and have babies. A breed is also a particular type of animal within a species.

breeder someone who raises animals

communication how animals talk to each other

descended born from. Children are descended from their parents and grandparents.

digest take food into the body

diurnal awake at dawn and dusk rather than night and day

domesticated living as pets rather than in the wild

dwarf a small type of an animal

food chain the links between different animals that feed on each other

forage to search for plants and food to eat

gnawing chewing, biting, or nibbling on something

groom to clean an animal, often with a brush

habitat where an animal or plant lives

herbivore animal that eats only plants

hierarchy the order that animals are in the groups

maggot the young of flies. They look like small, white wriggling worms.

mate when two animals come together to make babies

neuter operation to stop an animal from having babies

parasite tiny animals that live in or on another animal and feed off it

pests animals that breed in large numbers and cause damage

pika a member of the rabbit family that lives mostly in Asia

predator animal that hunts and eats other animals

sociable likes company and living in groups

species type of similar animals that can have babies together

vegetation groups of plants

Index